# The Pendant Project
## My Journey to Awareness Through Art

## Thurston Gray

The opinions expressed in this manuscript are solely the opinions of the author and do not represent the opinions or thoughts of the publisher. The author has represented and warranted full ownership and/or legal right to publish all the materials in this book.

The Pendant Project
My Journey to Awareness Through Art
All Rights Reserved.
Copyright © 2012 Thurston Gray
v2.0

www.thependantproject.com

This book may not be reproduced, transmitted, or stored in whole or in part by any means, including graphic, electronic, or mechanical without the express written consent of the publisher except in the case of brief quotations embodied in critical articles and reviews.

ISBN: 978-0-578-10462-1

Library of Congress Control Number: 2012905671

Published by Earth Bird Publishing
www:earthbirdpublishing.com

PRINTED IN THE UNITED STATES OF AMERICA

To every survivor
who has ever stood at a window,
staring at the stars,
and wished they didn't feel so alone.

# Acknowledgment

There are people who I need to thank. Joni, you found me, fed me and sheltered me when I needed it the most. You gave me Nemaha County and the good people in it. Todd, you gave me a safe place to breathe, rest, and be. Thirty six years of friendship and I still trust you. Marty, without you, I simply wouldn't be. You gave me the security and the open fields that helped me grow stronger. Reaca , Kathy taught me how to breathe but you made sure that I practiced, until I could do it naturally. Thank you for reminding me that I am creative, resourceful and whole. Peggy, meeting you at this point in my journey has been a wonderful gift. I can feel your hugs through the phone. Amy, your simple acceptance of me, as is, has been the catalyst to my healing. Thank you for your support, your humor and your love.

John, thank you. For years, you have watched me flit around, trying to find pieces of myself. It takes courage, patience and unconditional love to sit and allow me to do that. Thank you for your acceptance, support, strength, and love.

Cole, Blue, and Jack, Light, laughter and love came to my world when you entered it. Thank you for your unconditional love. I love you.

Logan Alanna and Ciara Brianne, I can't hold you in my arms but I always carry you in my heart.

# My Story

This project started as a whim. I had been playing around with Sculpey® clay, creating painted jewelry, when I read an article about Noah Scalin and his Skull-A-Day© project. For one full year, he created a skull, took a picture of it and posted it on his blog. Artistic, creative genius.

I wondered if I could do the same. Not with skulls, of course, but instead with the clay. I could use a cookie cutter to get a uniform shaped piece and use that as my guide. From there, I could do anything: draw, collage, paint, whatever. But the question was, could I really create 365 miniature works of art?

I challenged myself to do it. Yes, I would create a pendant a day for an entire year. I would keep a journal as well to document my thoughts about each piece. Simple enough.

Fortified with 30 pendants, baked and ready to go, a ton of old magazines, tubes of paint and a brand new spiral notebook, I created my first pendant on January 10, 2011.

Very quickly, The Pendant Project, as I had dubbed it, grew into something more. Something much, much bigger. *I made a rule.* Instead of simply creating a piece of wearable jewelry, I would, instead, document an emotion or feeling that I had experienced that day. That feeling I would then try to artistically represent on the pendant.

It is that change that sent me on this journey to awareness. The simple notion of identifying each and every emotion I felt throughout the day so I'd have something to "work with" at the end of the day is huge. Seriously, it was, and still is, life changing. Because if there is one area of me where I struggle the most, it is dealing with my emotions or feelings. For years I have either felt overwhelmed by them or I don't feel them at all. All or nothing. Black or white.

On October 14, 1988 I was raped.

At nineteen, I was a sophomore at my parents' alma mater. While they saw it for all its academic opportunities, I was there to experience life and freedom. I'd go to class during the week, then party all weekend long, sobering up just in time to do it all over again.

*He* was my boyfriend. A student/athlete, we had met about a month before through a friend of a friend. Usually, we'd meet at a party or bar and hook up from there.

That night it was the same; I got ready then caught a ride with my friends. Once at the bar, I found my boyfriend and said good bye to my girlfriends.

I woke up choking, gagging. On my back, I rolled my head to the side and I vomited at the feet and on the legs of a bunch of guys. I tried to move but my legs were pinned. Looking at them, I realized my shirt and bra were pushed up and my miniskirt was around my waist. I couldn't move my legs because they were being held open by a guy, a stranger, squatting between them.

"DANGER! DANGER! GET AWAY! GET AWAY!" screamed a voice in my head.

I tried. I fought the first three; bucking and twisting I tried to get away. Hands from every direction held me in place.

After seven, I stopped counting. I simply turned my head to the side and watched them watch me. The bed. The whoever guy whose turn it was.

Finally, they let me roll off the bed. I crawled to the door with them kicking, pushing and slapping me. Using the door as support, I got to my feet, stumbled down the hallway and ran down the stairs.

Four days later, the anger and outrage hit me. Hard. I grabbed a girl off my dorm floor; the only thing I knew about her was that she was strong and smart. And I needed back-up. So, with her, I went back to "the room", *his* dorm room, and confronted him.

"Why?" Why did you do that to me? Why did you let them do those things to me?" I screamed at him. He was sitting with two girls; the girlfriends I had caught a ride with that night. They, all three of them, laughed. He shrugged and said,

"You are a party girl and that night *you were the party.*"

With his statement, I assumed all responsibility for what had happened. It was my fault. I had done this. My world shattered. And in that instant, everything that I had ever thought about anything was completely destroyed. Shame, humiliation, pain, anger and shock overwhelmed me; everything turned white and I simply "checked out."

The next thing I remember, it was late December and I'm at my parents' house. My first day of awareness after the assault and I was filled with pain and grief. Alone, I cried all day long. I remember my mother calling me to dinner. Before I went upstairs, I stood in my bathroom. Looking in the mirror, I blew my nose, reapplied my makeup and tidied my hair.

The girl starring back at me was steely-eyed, determined. No one will ever know my shame; what had happened, what I did. No one. Not ever. *Whatever it takes.*

That day was the first day I put on my mask and pretended. Everything's great. I'm good. I. am. fine.

The world was different, foreign. I no longer understood it. It was like I was looking at it from a different angle; my view of it had shifted. My trust was shattered. I mean, *he* was my boyfriend. And my girlfriends had laughed – laughed. They weren't supposed to do that! That's not how I was taught to treat people. And the strangers, the other guys…where were they? I started looking for them everywhere. I became scared of everyone. That fear destroyed my confidence. I hadn't seen this attack coming, how would I stop the next one?

But I had to act the same. You know? I couldn't let anyone know I was terrified; I couldn't act scared or unsure. I couldn't cry or be sad. I would have to explain why and I couldn't say. Whenever those feelings overcame me, overwhelmed me, I would "check out." And pretend.

To carry on, I started to deny *it* ever happened. I built a closet in my head, threw it all in there and locked the door shut. I hid it from myself. It hurt way, way too much. I didn't know what to do with the feelings, the emotions I felt. They started to scare me as much as the "bad night" did. They were big, powerful and out-of-control. Best just to pretend, detach, and go numb, not feel anything.

That way I could go about my life, appear normal. I was "me." I did gradually change my wardrobe (no more miniskirts). I also changed my dorm room and my hairstyle. School became "important"; sorry can't make the party, I have a paper to write. I dropped all of my friends, I no longer trusted them. And I stopped drinking. By doing these things, I felt safer. And in control.

A little over a year later, I was walking to my first day of the spring semester. As I headed down the sidewalk to the building, I looked up. And saw *him*. I froze. He smiled and continued to walk towards me. Fear shot through my body. I couldn't breathe. And as he walked by me, he rubbed his body against mine. Suddenly freed from my trance, I ran into building, found the bathroom and threw up. I was late to class.

And so it began. Every Tuesday and Thursday, we'd play this sick game of hide and seek – trying to turn invisible, I'd silently beg – please, don't see me. He would smile and laugh. I think he liked seeing me shake and whimper. Because I *knew* what was coming! The knowing of what he would do to me messed with my head.

Soon he was everywhere. Not just bothering me on campus; he knew where I lived, knew my apartment, my car and my phone number. I couldn't get away from him. No place was safe for me anymore.

That's when the nightmares started. Vicious, terrifying dreams that would have me screaming aloud. I learned to be scared of the night and what it would bring. So I wouldn't allow myself to fall sleep. But when I was tired, I couldn't control the emotions that were always clawing at me. They'd start to break free and take over, ambushing me from every direction, while I'd desperately try to fight them all.

Losing that battle I looked to control something, anything. Food. I could control that; I decided what I ate, how much or if any at all. But even my eating disorder grew stronger than me.

That semester I lost everything again. Privacy, control, safety, trust. And I couldn't ask for help; didn't trust anyone enough to ask. And what would I tell them, anyway? I had never told anyone about the night I was raped, so who'd believe me now? I was alone to fight for myself. Instead, I spun down, around and around out-of-control into despair. *That* I clearly felt. I lost hope.

Losing hope makes a person do crazy things. Nothing is "off the table" of basic survival. Shit I never thought possible, never even contemplated, suddenly were the only options available. And I've done them. All. Alcohol to numb, sex for safety, pills to sleep, I have lied, manipulated, coerced and controlled myself and others to maintain my secret. And to keep all the feelings and emotions locked in the closet.

And while I had been great about shoving everything aside for years and years and *years*, I realize now that I was still "feeling" them. They simply showed up in a physical sense. I have had an all-over body rash, killer headaches, depression, ulcers and weird body sensations. Nightmares. I'm always unbelievably tired. All the time. But I can't relax enough to sleep. I'm jumpy. I startle easily. Do this little yelp sound. And I breathe funny. A pant-pant kind of breathing. Or I forget to breathe at all.

I got really good at pretending to the Outside World. I. am. fine. And, let's be honest, if you keep people at a distance, they don't notice your lies. Unless you were in my house, saw me without my mask, you would never know. Heck, there were times when even I forgot. I used to move a lot. Different city, different states. I changed my name. All of these changes helped me feel safe. And, yet, when I'd feel safe, my emotions and feelings would start to seep out. "Here I am," said my guilt. "Feel me," said my pain. No! I would deny them and distract myself.

It's not to say I've spent all these years totally dissociated. It's just that I'm unpredictable. Some days I'm there, fairly present, engaged in what's going on around me; I'm not pretending. Other days, I'm gone. Lost in my head, usually trying to control, beat back my emotions, feelings or *it*. Anger is the emotion I have the hardest time controlling. Doesn't take much to set me off, to trigger me.

Triggers are *everywhere*. In the media. Groups of men. Baseball games. Crowds of people. The smell of a berry wine cooler. The click of a seatbelt reminds me of the dorm room door opening. A Dr. Pepper can. Big things, little things, weird things, seemingly unrelated things, all have the power to send me back. Flashback.

That's where I was 4 years ago. The situation I was in, at the time, was totally and completely different than my assault. But the *feelings* I experienced were exactly the same. I had no control of my environment, I lost my personal space, and I was uneasy, unsure of myself – scared.

Suddenly, the past and present were mixed up, big time. Everything swirled together into this huge, overwhelming black mass of chaos. And the closet door in my head exploded open. Damaged beyond repair, nothing I tried worked at closing it. Desperate and despairing I realized I could lose everything. I could lose me, all over again. That was terrifying.

And I did something, at that moment that saved me, my life. I called out for help. I called the rape crisis hotline. The woman on the other end of the line listened to me. I was sobbing, mumbling, trying to speak and still she heard me. She gave me the number to the local center, encouraged me to call. And I did. After 18 years of silence – of pretending I was fine - I told my story. I wish I could say that after telling my story, everything got better. It didn't.

One of the first things my therapist did was help me rebuild the door to my "closet." Sounds crazy, right? We took everything, *everything* and shoved it back in. I shut the door and locked it tight.

She then asked me to visualize my safe place. *Not* the white room where I'm safe but numb, out of reach of everything but the place, full of color, where I can relax, breathe and feel. Describe that place.

*It's a meadow. The grass is kinda tall, golden in color. It slopes a bit, the meadow does. At the top of a slight crest there is a tree. A big, old cottonwood. It's huge, the trunk bigger than my arms are round. The branches, heavy with leaf, reach out, far, casting a dappled shadow at its base. Sometimes I curl up in between two roots that burrow deep into the earth, covered by my grandmother's quilt. In the quiet, I gently rub the gnarled bark. Other times, I spread the quilt out on the grass, out in the sun, and with the heat on my face, I watch the puffy clouds float across the blue sky and listen to the grasshoppers jump around.*

She asks me to remember, always remember I have that place. And it's okay to go there, at any time. It turns out, I needed that place. And every other "coping skill" I had ever acquired. Because we then reopened the closet door and started pulling stuff out.

Coping skills, I learned, were all the things I've done to get to this point, this day. Everything. Whether it was smoking, petting my dog, falling into a good book, "checking out," sleeping in or going on a walk. Every single action – the good, the bad, and the ugly – I took to get through the day or survive the night. They all had worth, value. They helped me survive my feelings.

I learned I had worth, too. I was valuable. And it wasn't my fault. It didn't matter what I wore, how I acted or how much I drank. It. Was. Not. My. Fault.

We talked about my childhood, introjection, dehumanization, victimization. We discussed PTSD; the symptoms and treatments of trauma, muscle memory, triggers, brain pathways, relationships, everything. I admitted my self-doubts, self-loathing, and my loneliness. I mourned my loss of safety, privacy and trust. And always, always I talked about what I was feeling.

At least I tried to. Sometimes there were simply no words. Just tears. Lots and lots of tears. Other times, I would be shaking, yelling and screaming, full of rage. And then there were the times, when in mid-sentence, I would just – poof – be gone. Back in the white room, out of reach of any pain.

But steely-eyed girl, full of determination was back. This time, though, I was ready to learn, to educate myself. I read books. I asked questions. I wanted resources; healthy, safe coping skills to help me deal when the "shit got bad."

I learned how to breathe. Deeply. *Sit upright. Breathe in through your nose – feel your tummy expand? – now, exhale through your month – your tummy contracts down.* That's a deep breath.

I learned how to "ground" myself. Come back to present time. *Sit upright again, put your feet flat on the ground. Now take a deep breath; inhale...exhale. Focus on your feet for a moment. Can you feel them touch the ground? How about your toes? Wiggle them. Feel them? What about your fingers? Can you feel them, too? Or do you need to rub them on your thighs? Okay, now blink. Look around the room. Where are you? Focus on the details. Are you back? Yes? Then good, you are grounded in the present.*

I joined a support group. Suddenly I was surrounded by people. Women. For the first time in *forever*, I was in a circle of women who understood. I didn't feel so alone. They got what I saying even when I couldn't speak the words, finish my sentence. They welcomed me. Listened, "witnessed" my experience, my struggle. So powerful that acceptance. I could be in a safe place, breathe, and simply be...me. No pretending. Wow.

Within the walls of that safety, I learned from them as well. Tentatively, I reached out, extending support and encouragement of my own. To them. I recognized strength and courage. Developed compassion and empathy, felt their pain, grieved their loss. Together, we rebuilt trust.

Awesome stuff. So uplifting. It filled me with hope. And that, in turn, gave me the fortitude to carry on. To really look at my experience, to feel my feelings and express my emotions. I would open the closet door, grab out something and hold it in my hands, so to speak. Turn it this way and that. Think about it, talk about it, process it. Maybe it was an actual part of my assault. Or maybe it was a judgment I felt in regards to something I'd done to survive. Regardless of whatever "it" was, I had to deal with it, incorporate, integrate it into who I am now.

For several years, I did just that. I showed up to each session, individual and group, present and willing. I made tremendous progress. I took steps, sometimes giant leaps, to healing my wounded soul. I worked hard…really, really hard. For three hours a week. Then I would shove it away until the next meeting.

Last January, when I changed the goal of The Pendant Project, that was my genius. Because it forced me to focus, every single, God damn day, on my self, my feelings and emotions. I couldn't really shove them aside if I had to recreate them on a pendant. The actual pendant, the art, made me accountable. My goal was a year, 365 days. Therefore, quite simply, I needed to have 365 completed pendants.

This project wasn't easy. But, really, nothing about the last 23 years has been. Head and heart work, in any form, requires strength, stamina, and an endless supply of courage. Pretending takes a ridiculous amount of energy. Why not apply all that energy into healing instead?

There are a million answers to that question. And everything single one of them is legit. For me, it was simply time. My inner voice said, "Now." And I listened.

I am tired of pretending, of saying every day "I'm fine". I'm not. I was raped. I may have healed from my physical injuries, but mentality, spiritually and emotionally, I am still recovering.

Living in the blinding white numbness or spinning into the black overwhelming chaos of emotion is exhausting. Somewhere, deep within my soul, I knew I didn't want live like that anymore. I wanted to live in a world full of color. The blue of sorrow, the yellow of joy, the red of passion… every color of life. To experience each emotion without becoming overwhelmed by them.

But I needed to change. Before I could do that, though, I needed to know what to change. And to figure that out, I had to pay attention. I had to be present. I had to be aware. What am I doing? Why am I doing it? Does it fit with who I am? Wait a second – who am I? I've been pretending for so long, I've lost sight of who I am.

All of that, taken whole, is a lot. But broken down into small steps – say, one day at a time – is manageable. Baby steps. When I feel something: pause, identify what it is, give it a name, hold it, then let it go. When I think about myself – of who I am, my values, beliefs, dreams – actually take the time and go beyond the surface.

The Pendant Project is the greatest gift I have ever given. Period. And, I gave it to myself. It's beautiful. From a strictly artistic point, each pendant, with its color, is a mini masterpiece. But when displayed together, it becomes this mosaic of a life fully experienced. My life authentically expressed.

And it's a gift I want to share. I picked out one hundred pendants, representing not just milestones in my journey, but also every day, ordinary days. Those little square art projects show how I see my feelings, my thoughts, my struggles and triumphs. But, I believe, you'll see yourself as well. There will be recognition. I have dealt with something that you, too, have experienced. There is beauty in a shared experience. It elevates. It soothes. It comforts. It gives hope.

*Thurston*

## January 10

Weave a New Fate –

I think this quote is appropriate. With the start of this endeavor, I'm going to create something new, one polymer clay project at a time. I'm excited to see how it goes.

## January 15

One of those days....I just wanted to get in the car and drive. I don't really care where the road goes so long as it never ends.....

## January 24

A blue horse running through the gray world. Black is the chaos; white is the numb. Gray is the space where I want to live, emotionally. I want to feel the serenity of blue, the passion of red, the grounding of brown and cheer of yellow. I want to experience every emotion without inhibition or judgment.

## January 27

Blank – I can't reach any emotions today; nothing. Not sure why and not wanting to "look"……

## February 1

Daydreams are a wonderful way to escape. To just imagine myself somewhere else, living some other life.

## February 2

Nest = Home

Bird = Mother

Egg = Child

A home should be a safe place. A place to nurture and strengthen the soul. Full of acceptance, support and unconditional love. My wish for all . . . .

## February 6

Phoenix – a bird in Egyptian mythology that lived in the desert for 500 years and then consumed itself by fire, later to rise renewed from its ashes. I haven't lived 500 years – I only look it and feel it most days – but it would be cool to rise renewed from the ashes of my old life.

## February 8

I love the process of mixing paints – blue, purple, black and white. Blop, blop, blop with the brush and what's created is an angry night sky. Rolling emotions; bubbling, brewing then CRACK! A burst of pure white electricity. Ahhh, the power! The lightning looks a bit like a woman dancing, hair flying, arms out reached in movement. Love it.

## February 9

I think one of the worst feelings I have is to not know where - in time- I'm at. The past seems so *today* that, sometimes, I get confused.

## February 12

I have sisters that I am bound to, not by blood, but, by experience. I share with them fear, loss, love, acceptance and support. It's these women that I forever carry in my heart.

## February 14

Today I feel horrible. My head hurts and I ache all over. I have a cold. My snarky, tongue-in-cheek pendant is a way to remember how important humor is!

## February 17

I tend to "dress the part." Whatever the environment or situation, I'll adjust my outfit appropriately. What I want is to blend in, for no one to notice me, leave me alone. If I feel invisible, then I feel relatively safe. The problem is I'm starting to want to dress for *me*. I want to find my style and wear it – regardless of whom I'm with or where I'm at. But I'm terrified to stand out, be noticed.

# February 19

I couldn't walk into a well-lit bar tonight. I was supposed to meet a friend, but she bailed. Knowing that I would be walking in, sitting, and listening to the band *by myself* completely freaked me out. The thing is I know this place! I know the layout, the exits, the crowd and, hell, even the owners and I still couldn't do it. I'm so pissed at myself. Pathetic.

# February 20

I'm a judgmental person. I try not to be but I'm not always successful. I judge how I look, how I feel and the choices I make. Especially the ones that I made years ago. Back then, I was a totally different person – the choices I made were based on my experience, knowledge and environment *then*. And yet I judge myself and those decisions based on what I know *now*. It's wrong, hurtful and very hard to stop. I long for the ability to just accept, to sit with compassionately, every choice I've ever made.

## February 24

Diamonds and pearls – a girl's best friend right? I love jewelry; the soft and delicate, the flashy and bold. All of it. But sometimes I wonder if I'm just trying to hide the ugly I feel. Look at the sparkly bling and not at me. Deflection at its finest?

## February 25

I entered an online competition today. I was to design and upload a photo that has a phrase or word written in lipstick that depicts what sexual exploitation looks like or feels like. I put a bar code on my breast and wrote "Not for Sale" in lipstick across it. It's a graphic, in-your-face image of exactly what is being sold. Sex. Tits and Ass. The actual person means nothing.

## February 27

I wish I could show who I am. I wish that I felt safe enough to just be me; to admit to the world that I am wounded, scared and lonely. But I don't and can't. Instead, I put on my mask and pretend I'm fine.

## March 3

When do I trust myself? Hard question. I can't say I always trust myself. But I am learning, slowly. I am really trying to listen to my intuition, my inner voice. My definition of intuition is my primitive brain processing everything (the conscious and unconscious) and leading me to do things certain ways – without understanding exactly why I'm doing it. Usually, I think, it's because of a threat – physical, emotional or mental. In the past, I would beat myself up for this but now I realize that these actions, that I do *intuitively*, have kept me alive. And that's a good thing.

## March 5

Last night at the Drag Queen Show, there was a table reserved for a birthday party. Twenty-two people showed up at 9pm on a Friday night for the guy's birthday. I can't even name 22 people, let alone invite them to my party. The people that sat at that table were young, older, gay, straight, men and women. And all of them had a deep enough connection to Birthday Boy to show up. Watching the group, I felt envious, isolated and lonely. And a whole lot sad because I think I'm the one missing out. All because I'm afraid to let people into my life, to trust.

## March 10

Anticipation, excitement, nervous are words that describe what I'm feeling today. My stomach is fluttery and I'm having a hard time staying completely grounded. Tomorrow I have a big, scary, totally-out-of my-comfort-zone meeting. Yikes! I'm freaked but determined! I'm going to do it! Yeah Me! Makes me think of doors opening, possibilities and new directions….

## March 17

Had a discussion about boundaries today. Social boundaries versus personal boundaries. Physical, sexual, emotional boundaries. How often does my personal space bubble change? Hourly? Daily? Who I am with? Where I'm at? What happens to me when my boundary is crossed? How do I respond? Feel?

I don't think I've ever really thought about boundaries, my boundaries. They are just there to keep me safe. But this conversation made me think; do my boundaries need to be adjusted? And how do I do that and still feel safe?

## March 25

Hello, Book. Beautiful friend that's going to take me places and introduce me to new people. At 13, I learned the true gift of a book. While I was reading, I could either stuff the bad shit totally away, in my head, with the door locked or I could leave it cracked just a bit, allowing the bad stuff to squeeze out in small, manageable – process-able - amounts at a time. I still have that book, the one that saved me all those years ago. And I still hold dear the value of being able to "get away" for a while. Thank you, Book.

## March 28

I am not dumb or stupid. I just don't understand. I don't understand how guys that would never rape a woman on their own would join in a group rape, a gang rape. Why? I don't get it. And I can't find any information that adequately explains it to me. That's what I usually do if I have questions; I research, study and find the answers. But for this? Nothing I read gives me the answers I need. And that worries me. I'm scared the lack of answers will trigger me into feeling dumb and stupid. I'm not. I. Just. Don't. Understand.

## April 1

Sunny, bright, cheerful and peaceful. That is how I feel today. I spent the day outside digging in the garden. I felt the damp soil, letting it fall through my fingers. I watched the clouds drift across the blue sky and I listened to the birds sing their songs of life. I sat there, grounded and content.

## April 5

Like physical labor, internal work is HARD! Finding authenticity in my actions is difficult. Acknowledging, changing or giving up survival behaviors is a slow, scary process. Nothing happens overnight (except for trauma — amazing how fast *that* can occur.) Dripping water on a rock will change its shape, over time. Just remember to be patient, kind, present and aware. Change will happen!

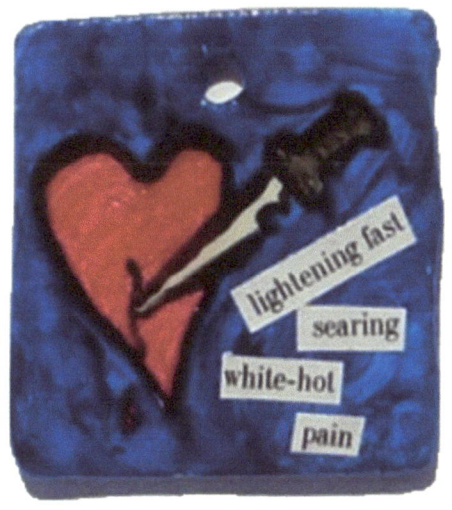

## April 12

I made a decision years ago. It was painful, but right for me, at the time. Today, the phone rang. Caller ID sent me straight to hell. The pain of my past was like a flash of white lightning - white hot, red hot — searing through my heart. I gasped and stepped away from the phone only to fall off a cliff into dark, deep grief, sorrow, and mourning. Why call me after all this time? Twisting the knife so deep into my heart. Alone in the kitchen, I bawled. It was the right choice so why won't the pain stop??

## April 14

The Recovery. I woke up breathing. To which I rolled my eyes. Really? Again? It just seems to happen every day; I wake up. So, today, I'm going to try. Try some self-care, try some self love. Yesterday I acknowledged the grief I carry. Today, I am going to acknowledge that I am resourceful and strong. I am going to use my resources, going to reach out for them and soothe myself into deep breathing.

What I have felt the last three days is real, authentic and ok. Hear that? My feelings are OK!

## April 16

Today I was "outed" as a survivor by an agency that should know better. My personal privacy – my choice to share – was one of the biggest things I lost that night. I now take privacy, mine and that of others, incredibly seriously. I should be offended, freaked, or totally outraged, yet I'm not. I want to be able to acknowledge; to say it myself, "I am a sexual assault survivor." Out loud and even if my voice shakes.

## April 21

The shit I have endured (*endured* … I hate that word, it's like the worst word ever) in life has made me the person I am today. No doubt about it. The choices I made after those experiences have been the driving force in how I got where I am today.

I want to acknowledge – just for a moment –courage, inner strength, determination, cleverness, and hope. Not words I normally use to describe myself but all qualities I have. All stuff you need to go from victim to survivor.

## April 24

A loss can be so big that one's heart simply breaks.

My heart broke over my loss of safety. The world's a scary place for me now. My heart broke for my loss of privacy. Every part of me was violated. Today I guard all aspects of my world with consistent vigilance and thought. My heart broke over the loss of my control. I did not choose what happened to me – not one thing. My heart broke for the choices I did have to make, to simply survive. Decisions that continue to haunt me today.

My heart is still broken, missing pieces that can never be put back together again…

## May 1

"Justice has been done" was all over the media today. I was curious to just what the word "justice" really meant so I looked it up in the dictionary. According to Webster's, justice means a reward or penalty as deserved. Today's justice was for the men, women and children lost in September 11th terrorist attacks.

I wonder if the families left behind feel any different, did today's justice bring relief, closure, or just more emptiness. They will never get to hold their loved one again, regardless. They still have an enormous hole in their hearts. Does it get better because justice was served?

## May 2

I drive this particular route twice a week. Today, half way through my trip I got lost. I simply looked around and could not figure out where I was or where I was going. And in that second of being "lost," everything came back. The feelings of running scared, he's following me – run, run, faster! – Oh God, he's gonna get me –hide, hide quick!

I still hear his breathing, feel my fear.

I found my way home but I'm still shaking, still can't catch my breath. I absolutely hate this! Hate. It.

## May 3

After that feeling of being lost yesterday, I know I should rebuild. Remind myself that even when I get lost, I can find my way back. I am strong; I've done this before, I can do it again.

I had to work on my front yard. My creepy neighbor was also out. So, I'm outside, by myself, and I can feel him watching me. "He" becomes abstract and I'm triggered into "they" are watching me. I feel like I'm being stalked, hunted, again.

Can't stay present. Back and forth in my head. I have enough self awareness to know that I'm reacting to yesterday's trigger and that it's blurring with today's but I still want to run, hide anything – just get away.

## May 11

I started doodling and this is what appeared. A little creepy, a little sad. I understand the sadness. The headstone – not so much. I used to wander old cemeteries, reading the headstones. I would think about the people buried. Who knew them? Were they loved? Are they missed?

I wonder if I'd be missed...

## May 14

I spent the entire evening giving myself a complete manicure and pedicure. It was wonderful! The entire process of bathing, drying, lotion then doing my nails was just what I needed. To connect with my body, care for it. To connect to and care for *myself*.

## May 17

I went to my favorite Indie bookstore. It's more than just books, gems, charms and music though, it's a spiritual oasis. I feel completely protected the moment I walk through the doors. Today, I needed to be surrounded by love. I needed a hug of acceptance and a smile of understanding. And in that circle, I was able to get my bearings and catch my breath.

## May 19

Mandala – inside the circle of the mandala is a view of me. Born in Nature, I am the earth of the mountains, the water of the river, fire of the sun, and the breath of air. I am loyal and strong like Horse; fragile yet adaptable like Dragonfly; creative and magical like Crow; and honor life like Buffalo.

## May 22

An FE4 tornado hit Joplin, Missouri today. It's being rated as the single most deadly tornado recorded. Devastation is complete. Everything and lots of good people are simply gone. The TV is showing some of the survivors – I've seen their look before. The shock, numbness, blank stares are reflections of what I've seen in my mirror.

I think that's the thing about trauma. While each person's event may be different, the effects are the same. Grief, anger, sleeplessness, denial, fear, guilt and thankfulness will all have to be acknowledged, processed and integrated into the "new normal." Hard work under trying times. I am so sorry for your losses, Joplin.

## May 23

I am triggered today. I am so annoyed at damn near everyone! Stupid people are pissing me off, big time! Petty things, inconsiderate people – grate on my nerves. I know one of the reasons I am annoyed is because I have been thinking about the tornado victims. And I know, firsthand, that the world doesn't stop just because you're hurting. It doesn't allow time for you to catch your breath, or develop a plan or find a safe place. Instead, bills pile up, landlords start yelling and bosses don't understand. Old life collides with new life.

I know where the survivors are right now and I'm annoyed at the world on their behalf.

## June 3

Contempt. Apparently in my desire to protect myself, I have elevated myself above all others. I sneer at their very existence. I devalue their very presence (however minimal) in my life. To know I choose to dehumanize others when I feel threatened is an ugly reality in the mirror.

It's not enough that I am aware I do this, I must change my behavior. Otherwise, how different am I from them?

## June 6

I care now. And that is all that matters.

## June 15

Big day, today. For the first time since my assault, I can go into the "room" and have no reaction. I'm not fearful; I don't feel dread or am I anxious. The only thing that I feel, really, is a sense of sadness. I lost so much that night! For that, I grieve. But I am not terrified of the men in the room or the pain they can inflict. I'm not trapped or tied down anymore. I remember the pain, but I no longer feel it, live it.

I wish I had the energy to jump and shout, to dance in freedom and survival. Instead, I gather myself close and hold the girl I once was and the woman I've become.

## June 18

The world seems different. I'm not sure how it's different, I just feel like I'm looking at it in a different way. My view of it has tilted, again. And I'm tired. Unbelievably tired. Exhausted. Yet, when I try to sleep, my body just revs. I feel like my brain is humming…no thoughts…just turned up high. I have a million things to do; my daily list keeps growing and, yet, all I want is to sleep. Really sleep.

## June 22

Ok, I admit, I thought things would be different. Somehow, magically, all of my fears and freaky behaviors would just drop away and I'd be me, my old self, my before self. Apparently, that's not how this works.

Everything is off today. I can't get my bearings. I am trying to pause and think my way through my decisions. So, I stop and think…and can't make a decision at all. I simply don't know anything about anything. I can't even decide if that's good or bad.

## June 23

Here's the thing about staying silent. If you don't share the bad experiences then you really have nobody to share the good ones with, either. I have one close friend. She knows my story. She has seen me crawl, beaten and bloodied from the deepest depths of despair. She knows how hard it's been for me to pretend I'm fine. To hide my triggers and live a "normal" life.

I told her where I'm "at" today. She's so happy for me! The two of us did a little happy dance. It was wonderful to have someone to acknowledge and celebrate my survival with. Because today, I can finally say I survived.

## June 29

I found the most amazing quote on a greeting card. Like a gift from the universe, it was exactly the affirmation I needed today.

So many times I hear only the negative voices in my head. Yelling and screaming at me for all my mistakes and failures. Instead, I need to stop and listen. Really listen because beneath all the noise, I hear my husband, my best friend, my therapist and most importantly, myself.

If I really, really listen I can actually hear myself. How cool is that?

## July 3

It occurred to me today that I require an ungodly amount of space; emotional, mental, and physical. I know it's a boundary thing; I am aware and working on it. What's appropriate? How do I discuss my concerns? Blah, blah, blah.

How come I can scream, quite clearly, in my head, "Give me some space!" but I can't say them out loud? Instead, I let the "suffocating" pressure just build and build until I'm completely triggered. Ugh.

## July 5

Thoughts of freedom... How many of us do not have the opportunity to take off our masks and simply be accepted for who we are? How many of us are too frightened by the thought of rejection and exposure to even try?

I think expectations are learned very quickly and at an early age. Through tone of voice, a look or demand, we learn how important it is to meet someone's expectation. We also learn how painful disappointment, disapproval and consequences can be. Many times it's simply easier to meet someone else's standards than to meet our own. We learn how to throw aside our own wishes, plans or feelings.

In the short term, I have found it to be the best way to respond. Just get through it and deal with the personal cost later. The problem I'm finding is that automatically meeting other's expectations, at the cost of my own, adds up. I feel it in the tightness of my chest, in my difficulty of taking a deep breath, in the fatigue I feel. It takes an enormous amount of energy to live someone else's view of my life.

## July 7

What is trust? Intellectually, I know that a relationship built on trust includes respect, reliability, risk, honesty, acceptance, consistency and forgiveness.

I guess when I have all of that then I feel *safe*, I relax then I feel like I can *breathe*. After taking a deep breath, I feel *present*. I am grounded which allows me to acknowledge my many emotions and tell the *truth*. Ultimately, I feel *authentic* when I'm with someone I trust.

## July 9

I like my anger, a lot. Sometimes, I flash burn. I'm seemingly fine then POW I simply explode. Other times, I will simmer – on high – all day. I grab onto the anger and don't let go. If I feel like it's softening, I will feed it. I'll think of other slights, other times when I been angry and add them to the fire. Then I can rage, "justified," all day.

Anger is a good emotion. It's in us to protect us. Our anger is a result of a boundary violation. Anger propels us to fight, to protect.

My anger definitely protects me. Everyone scatters when I get angry. I require lots of space and I get it. But that's all I get; me and my anger. Because once I grab on to the anger, I can't hold any other emotion. Not happy, not sad, not content, nothing else.

I need to learn, desperately want to learn how to say "Hello anger, I feel you." And I hug it close and then I let it go. Feel it then let it go. Fluidity not flames. Sounds simple enough in theory but it's going to require practice, practice, practice.

## July 11

I am working on fluidity of emotions again today. Emotions are like water. They flow throughout my body, my being. I have no idea how many times I've read this or been told it. "Just *sit with* whatever I'm feeling." Let them simply pass through me.

It's very uncomfortable to sit with embarrassment or shame or guilt. I can maybe sit for 3 or 4 minutes, tops, before I start to squirm around. Then I shove the feelings away. "Cork" my emotions. But I also feel a sense of accomplishment for enduring them for the few minutes I had them out. For that small amount of time, I felt them. And that's a good start.

## July 12

Thunderstorms tonight. Lots of thunder and lightning. My dog, Katie, is scared of the loud sounds. I know this because Katie does not wear a mask. I know how close a storm is by watching her. Her ears go back, she tucks her tail and she'll belly crawl to her kennel. She's frightened and she shows it.

There's no pretense with Katie. She hasn't learned, like me, to cover her fears. She hasn't learned to pretend. To smile when her stomach is rolling, to laugh when instead she wants to cry at the hurtful words, to stand still when she's hearing run, run in her head.

Katie lives in the present. All animals do, except for humans. The authenticity of her actions/behaviors to her emotions is something I admire. I only wish I could be as true to myself and my feelings. (And, I am working on it.)

## July 17

I am grateful. I have a friend, my best friend, who is always there for me. And just as important I am there for her.

I think that is what makes our friendship work. We are both reliably consistent. If I say I'll be there, I am. She does the same. I respect her, her views and honesty. I am always honest with her. I love her and accept her for who she is at this moment, right now. And I can forgive her, if I need to. All of this is a description of trust. I simply and completely trust her.

And that is why I am grateful for her presence in my life. She has given me the most amazing gift, the opportunity to trust again.

## July 18

Here's the story of a circus lion. He grows up in a 10 x 10 foot cage. All he does, every day, is pace from one end of the cage to the other. Step, step, step. Along comes a wildlife rescue group. They rescue him from his tiny cage. The lion can't be released to the wild so they build him a huge habitat. An entire acre for the lion to roam and play in.

But what does the lion do in his new space? He paces… step, step, step. Even though he has freedom to move around, he only takes three steps. Because that is all he knows. Learned behavior. Now the lion has to learn new behaviors in his new life.

I feel like the lion. I've been freed a bit by all the work I have done; yet I still do the same stuff, behave the same way. Why? Because it's my learned behavior! I am aware that the boundaries of "my cage" have changed but I'm having a hard time navigating in this new world of mine.

It's frustrating and hard! I don't think I'm giving myself the patience that I would give the lion. I understand it would take time, days, months, years even, for him to adjust. Why? Why? Why can't I give myself the same love, patience and understanding?

## July 25

I already know that shopping is not going to fill up the empty spot inside me. Nor will "blowing something up" or trying to close the closet door in my head and pretend.

The answers are within me. If I would simply stop, look and listen to my own voice, I would hear the voice of my soul telling me what I need.

What I lack is confidence. For too many years I listened to their voices, telling me how to behave, who I should be and how little I'm worth.

Enough! I'm tired of it. No matter how hard it is to stop and listen, I'm going to try. I have dreams, desires and I damn know that I have value. So, every single day I am going to listen to myself, tune out the "others" and discover all the things that will fill me up. Stop, listen and look inside.

## July 26

Laughter is the sound of the emotion of happiness. Today, I laughed a lot. Out loud. I felt happy. I watched AFV – I love that show! It's hilarious! I am confident that nothing makes me connect to my emotion of happiness faster than watching an old lady try to run down a steep hill. Oh God, the visual! Even now, I'm still laughing! Poor woman, I hope she wasn't hurt when she cartwheeled….

It should be a prescribed treatment plan for everyone; find a show that makes you laugh and watch it faithfully.

## July 31

I am going to make a judgmental comment here and say that today was not my most productive day. The one and only thing I accomplished was doing a single load of laundry. Woo hoo.

This, of course, means that for the next couple of days I will run around and try to compensate. Busy-busy. Trying to make up for my lost day.

I know that self awareness is the first step to correcting behavior. I just wish it was the only step...

# August 2

Today I received some bad news. I immediately felt the rise of injustice, followed closely by anger which morphed into rage. Bam! Just like that, that fast.

I just as quickly took a deep breath and literally said, out loud, "This is my rage. I will hold it gently in my hands." Breathe in…breathe out.

I then did and said the same thing for my anger and feeling of injustice.

It worked, in that I didn't rage the rest of the day. I got upset. I acknowledged my feelings and then I let them go. Tonight, I feel proud. I felt myself getting disproportionately angry and I did something about it, in a respectful and gentle way. I am listening to myself and being aware of my feelings. I'm also really learning to treat myself with compassion.

## August 4

Ugh. Tonight my emotions are bouncing all over the place. Anger, nervous, distraction, happy, sad. Just like a ball in a pinball game. Ping, ping, ping.

I want to grab one and (gently, of course) hold it. But I can't; they are moving around too fast. While it's uncomfortable, I am still grateful. I can individually identify them as they zip around; they haven't gelled into overwhelming chaos. Yet. It's time to ground!

## August 5

Tonight I attended a sold-out concert. I was nervous about how I would respond to the crush of people. I typically avoid crowds. People who've been drinking. I've been a bit "twitchy" just thinking about it.

But you know what? I did fine. Yes, there were a couple of times when I felt trapped – but it was a flash – and I was able to breathe through it. The concert was great and I enjoyed myself. Yeah Me!

## August 10

I am so angry! Burning mad! I am outraged at the injustice I witnessed by a school and its district today. As the day goes on, and my anger simmers, I realize I am triggered. It's been a while. I think the way the school denounced the value of their student; the "unworthiness" of the child is the fuse that lit my fire.

Instead of receiving encouragement, empowerment and support; the child was left floundering on his own. That's the cause of my anger. That sense of abandonment by someone who should be supportive, who should guide and protect. How dare they? Despicable.

I feel outrage, hurt, offended, empathy, and so sorry for the kid.

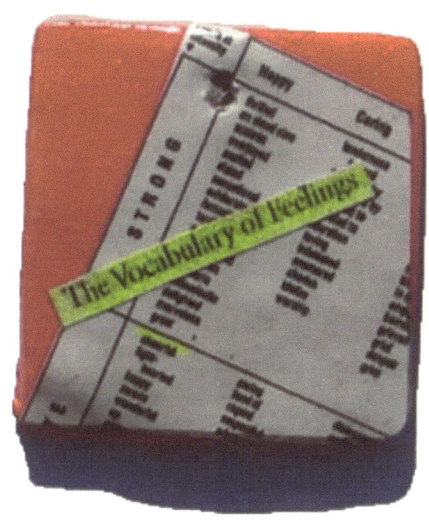

## August 18

I was given the gift of words today. Specifically, the "Vocabulary of Feelings" chart. It's a table which shows the ten major emotions then breaks them down in intensity – strong, moderate, mild feelings.

Why am I just now receiving this list? This knowledge? My answer is that today is the day that I am ready to learn and speak more authentically.

Trauma took away my ability to speak. Just like a child learning to talk, when I regained my voice, I would use simple words – good, bad, fine, horrible. Now, finally, as I grow in learning to listen to my feelings and to verbalize them, my vocabulary gets to grow as well.

Today, I have a new word. Cheerful. I feel cheerful.

# August 24

"What will the neighbors think?" was a question that ruled and guided my childhood. The statement "Don't do anything to embarrass the family" was always thrown at me as I left the house to hang out with my friends in high school.

I thought that I had left the judgment of those words behind me. Turns out, not completely.

I am hesitant to post pictures of my awesome weekend feat. An event that I am so proud I did. Yet I worry about how "others" will view me.

Will they think I'm crazy (in a bad way), ridiculous? Fat? Ugly? When I view the pictures I see myself having fun, happy, and determined. Smiling, I am completely covered in mud.

Why can't I risk sharing this achievement with them? Do I really trust so little?

## August 30

I can't begin to explain what this pendant means. However, I can say that I found Karen McLaren's book, *The Language of Emotions – What Your Feelings Are Trying to Tell You* life changing.

## August 31

This morning I wrote a letter to the universe. In it, I listed my dreams for my future. Actually, it's more a letter of intention. My dreams are really my goals, ones I will achieve. By putting them on paper, I feel I have validated their importance. My importance.

I can now make up an action plan, so to speak, of steps, baby steps, I can take to manifest my dreams.

I am excited! I plan to do some pretty incredible things!

## September 4

Today I intentionally avoided thinking and feeling. I purposely kept everything at the surface level. I know it's called avoidance. I know this. But I simply didn't feel strong enough, grounded enough to let my emotions "flow." I felt a real sense of being overwhelmed so I detached, dissociated and avoided everything.

## September 5

Everything that I avoided yesterday was here to greet me today. Funny how that works. Today, though, I didn't avoid my feelings. I was tired, irritable, grumpy, weepy and sad, unbelievably sad.

Sad is what I was avoiding yesterday. Not the overwhelming, debilitating kind of sad but more just a constant ache in my heart.

I identified sad. I acknowledged sad. I felt sad. I held my sadness. And, today, I was able to breathe through it.

Pain + Resistance = Suffering

## September 9

I feel smug. I was able to pull myself out of a death spiral. Yesterday, I bombed a presentation. It went so horribly that midway through it I had a panic attack. God awful, wretched experience. And that threw me spinning.

But, today, I was able to pause and breathe. Really breathe. Then I was able to refocus – ground – myself and actually acknowledge my anxiety. I was able to tell myself that it's ok to feel anxious and mean it. Then I just Let. It. Go.

Four or 5 months ago, I would not have been able to do that. Instead, my anxiety would have mushroomed into a big Ugly and it would have taken me days, weeks, even, to return.

So, I am celebrating. I feel happy, a little boastful, and a bit more confident in my skills at "returning to center."

# September 10

I remember walking into an airport 15 minutes before my flight. I remember never having my purse screened before a concert or football game. I don't remember even thinking once about a school or mall being a "soft target."

That's the thing about a traumatic event. It forever changes the view of your world and the way you act in it. Before and After.

I still remember my "'before." I remember the things I wanted to do, the places I wanted to see. What personal safety issues? Nothing's going to happen to me. I remember how I felt – confident, sure of myself. The risks I took! The entire world was mine and I was going to experience it. I was spontaneous and outgoing. I would meet new people and try new things.

Then, my world shifted. My "after" looks radically different. The entire world I desired shrank to an 1800 sq ft house that I don't leave after dark. When I do go out, it is with a plan. And a backup plan. I look for escape routes and items I can use as weapons.

I avoid groups or gatherings of people. If I have to attend, I stay on the outskirts and do nothing to get noticed. My faith and trust has been crushed.

Ten years, 20 years. It doesn't matter how much time has passed. Things will never be the same again. Before and After.

## September II

For the last three years, I have participated in a 9/11 Memorial Stair Climb. Climbers honor and remember the first responders by climbing 110 stories. I, personally, don't climb just for them, but rather for all of the victims of the terror attacks.

In the parking lot, I came across these bottle caps. I felt they really represented all victims, and survivors, of violence. It does not discriminate. Corporate workers or entrepreneurs, men, women, and children of every nation bear witness to the brutality of violence. It can strike any time, any place in many different ways.

And just like drops of water on a pond, the effects of violence ripple out, touching all who care. Not only are the survivors forever changed, but the friends and family, spread across nations, are affected as well.

## September 15

I am totally freaked. Overwhelmed, tired, scared, sad and weepy. In this moment, I feel so helpless.

And I'm terrified that this moment will blend into my next moment and into my next moment until that's all I am. Helpless and hopeless.

## September 16

No chance to catch my breath…I feel wounded and weak. Danger is coming. I must protect myself.

I put on my mask. It is firmly in place. My emotional survival depends on my acting ability. I must appear ok. Everything's normal. Everything's fine. I. Am. Fine.

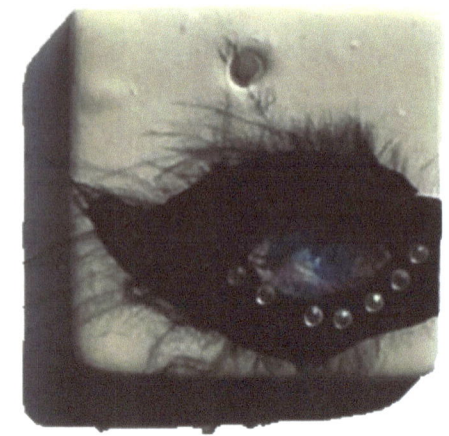

## October 1

So hopeful today. In fact, I made a Bucket List. First time for that! I wrote down all kinds of things – goofy, ridiculous, outrageous things that sound absolutely fun to do. Laugh out loud. I'm so excited. I really must keep this pendant handy to remember how I feel today, because... I feel marvelous!

## October 2

Paper dragon or real one? It used to be I couldn't tell the difference. I would respond to any danger as a legitimate threat to my person. I would remove it (or myself) by any means possible.

I have come to the realization that I now have this ability to pause – just for a second - and evaluate whether the danger is genuine danger, life threatening, or if rather the person or situation simply makes me uncomfortable. Those ones, I call paper dragons. They look real but aren't. They make me feel unsafe, thus, triggering my fear.

The fact that I have developed this awareness to pause and process is amazing. It really speaks to the hard work I'm doing.

## October 3

I am so pumped! I have this idea and I finally have figured out how to make it work. Go big or go home, right? Well, this is big in my world. It's going to take me in a wonderful new direction, full of light, power and pride.

I admit I admire my courage, determination, and creativity today.

## October 10

I went back into the "room" today. I stood above the bed and looked around. I looked at every single guy in the room. I also looked at the bed and me on it.

I took slips of paper and wrote their name (or description) on it. Then I went to the fireplace. As I lit each paper on fire, I said "I forgive you." And I watched the paper burn. One paper caught flame, then another and another until, finally, I was left with just one name.

I held my lighter to the last paper and said aloud, "I forgive myself." It will only be after I forgive myself, let go of judgment, that I will truly be free; free from my past, free to accept and free to love myself.

## October 11

Overwhelming sadness today. I feel it throughout my body; my chest is heavy and tight, my head hurts and I feel cold. I have no appetite and no energy. Just this huge heaviness bearing down on me. At first, I didn't even realize I was crying. I tried to stop them, slow them down. Instead, more came. Soon I was sobbing. With my sobs came the pain. I feel so much pain! I hurt so badly.

Nothing hurts worse than losing one's self.

## October 12

I have spent this past year trying desperately to acknowledge, feel and accept my feelings, my emotions. And while I sometimes get frustrated at my baby steps, I really have come into a deeper awareness of my self.

But yesterday's intense grieving rattled me. "Sitting with" so much pain and sorrow left me breathless.

So, today, without judgment, only compassion and lovingkindness, I am focusing simply on breathing, slow, deep mindful breaths.

Inhale…exhale…inhale…exhale…

## October 14

Woke up two hours late this morning, humming the Happy Birthday song. For lunch, I ate a most delicious gourmet raspberry cupcake.

It's not my birthday. It is the anniversary date of the day I was raped. Usually a day full of flashbacks, pain and fear; this day, today, feels different.

I physically do not hurt. I am not nervous, anxious, or frightened. I am not looking over my shoulder for an ambush or feeling watched.

I am present and grounded. I feel really good. "Free" is not an emotion, per se, but it definitely describes how I feel. I am free.

## October 16

Experience counts. I think that's why support groups are so effective. Each member has a different path to the group but once we all get together, our experiences are the same. The violence, the dehumanization, the helplessness, the pain; we have all experienced those. And afterwards, the anger, the fear, the numbness - the fall out is the same too.

Perhaps, we reach different emotions or reactions at different times, but we all cycle through the same healing process.

My support group is where I am heard and understood, where I feel safe, where I can breathe and where I can heal.

It's my wish to the universe that every survivor has the same in their group.

# October 24

BAM BAM BAM

The angry voices are back. Actually, it's only one voice, mine, telling me "you're stupid. Dumb. Who do you think you are? You can't do this! You're not creative or smart! You can't do anything right!" Over and over again all day long.

These thoughts totally paralyze me. I literally can't do anything because I'm scared I'll mess up. So, I just sit, listening.

## November 2

Everyone is different. How we look, talk, and learn is as unique as how we think, feel and heal.

I have been so blessed to find three amazing, remarkable women – goddesses, really – who have each in their own creatively different ways encouraged and supported me in my healing journey.

Their strength is their awareness of where I am "at" and how they engage me in this process of self-discovery and acceptance. Each one of them has truly made me feel accepted for who I am while pushing me to increase my boundaries. Their mastery of connecting with survivors cannot be taken for granted. They simply save lives.

From the very depths of my soul, I thank them for each connecting with me in their own authentic way to walk with me down my personal path.

## November 6

There is a lot of discussion about Fairy Tales. How they are told, what they mean and the messages sent to young girls. All very valid arguments.

But I'm going to focus on the hope that fairy tales give me. The notion that after everything endured; good will still triumph over evil. By simply believing in the magical, opportunities never before dreamed will come true. It's a lovely premise.

I know I have hope. True, it may be an itty, bitty flame struggling against the wind but it's still there. It is hope that helps me get up every day, determined to face my emotions and accept them as is, without judgment or denial.

And that courage, strength and grace is as beautiful as any princess.

## November 10

My nightmares are back. Bummer. But today, I did something different. I took a deep breath and replayed it in my head. And as I did, I wrote everything down.

I then read it aloud. I described how I felt in the dream; the fear, the cold, the terror in him catching me. I talked about the sound of his breathing and mine, the squeak of the opening door. I read about what I saw; the cement stairs, the pine trees. All of it. In hideous, terrifying detail.

Usually after a "bad night" I feel the residual effects. I can't get warm, I'm tired and scared. But today, I realized that while I was reading my nightmare aloud, I knew it wasn't happening, currently. I felt the fear but it was a sort of remembered fear. My feet were cold but I could still feel them touching the ground.

Basically, what I'm saying is that I could retell my nightmare without falling back into it. And that made me feel very powerful.

## November 12

I listened to a CD today on manifesting my future. Visualizing my future.

In my mind's eye, I walked around my farm. To the south of the property, there is a wooded area, perfect for a small cottage. By the big house, there is a barn, a shed building that I use as a studio and a brightly colored chicken coop.

When I walk into the house, I immediately hear laughter. Drawn to the kitchen, I find it full of family and friends. And as I glance out the kitchen window, I see two horses munching on grass in the pasture.

By the end of the CD, I felt really good, deeply breathing, and fully believing that I will be able to manifest this life I long for.

## November 17

I get lost a lot. I look around and don't know where I am. My new wrist tattoo is of a compass. It's a visual reminder to myself that whenever I am feeling lost, to stop and look inside. I have the answers (or directions) inside me. All I need to do is listen. When I do that, I'll hear my voice telling me how to get back home.

## November 23

Aha moment today.

There is no "instant new life" or magic pill that makes things happen. Instead it is making a choice, a positive, conscious choice. And doing it over and over again. Day after day. It's *time* that gives you the results.

I have been taking baby steps, acknowledging my emotions one day, one pendant at a time. Well, over the course of a year, I will have made 365 pendants or, another way to look at it, I will have acknowledged my emotions 365 times. That's huge!

I get discouraged because I don't always feel like I am making progress, yet, today I really understand how much growth I have achieved. Simply because I did it day after day, pendant after pendant.

## November 27

Oh what fun I had today! I made jewelry. I used gem stones, crystals, metal and clay to make fabulous charms for my necklace. While shopping for supplies, I found some inspiring ink stamps; I am playing with them as well.

This break from the norm is exactly what I needed. I feel crafty and creative again. I have tons of ideas floating around in my head. Exciting!!

## November 28

I admitted before that humor is important for everyone, especially, I think, for survivors. Humor and the ability to laugh were the first things to go after my assault. The world was a scary place and meant to be taken seriously. True. And humor – just finding that one thing funny – can be so uplifting.

I am learning again to laugh with my friends. We tease, cut jokes and make smart ass comments to each other. We laugh at ourselves and each other. The perfectly timed remark can take a super serious, incredibly painful moment and lighten it, just enough to catch our breath. And that is truly magical.

I don't ever want to lose my sense of humor again. A world without the chimes of laughter is such a bleak, despairing place.

# December 2

I think it's one of my biggest regrets – not being stable enough to be a foster/adoptive parent.

I am aware of issues surrounding my own adoption. The feelings of abandonment, of not being "loveable" and also of not fitting in to my adoptive family, being an outsider. I think the worst feelings I have center around the idea that I may be "sent back" to wherever I came from. Don't mess up, don't make a mistake. Scary.

I think perhaps many of my assault issues are mixed up with my adoption issues. It's just so hard and overwhelming to try to separate them; it's not even possible. I know that how I responded to my assault was in accordance to the beliefs I held of my childhood. So, I just try to work on one part at a time. Small manageable pieces of a much bigger pie.

## December 8

Awhile back I took a temperament test. Today, I got the results back. All I could think as I was told was, "that's not me!"

So I re-read the temperament book, retook the test and then figured out, myself, how to read the results and scored myself.

I scored exactly the same numbers. Exactly. Apparently, that is me, after all.

For the second time in one day, I read the temperament book. I realized that many of the explanations of behavior did, indeed, fit me. The news was a bit unnerving yet, comforting, in a weird way. Meaning that while I am uniquely me, I still fit in the parameters of known behavior. And, *that*, my friends, is always good to know.

## December II

Everyone pulled me in different directions today. Need this, do that.

Sometimes, I can handle it, thrive with it – snap, snap – watch me do it all. Other days, like today, it's a trigger. Pulling me this way, tugging on me that way. I started to feel like fighting, like I have to claw my way through them.

Instead of saying anything, though, I just go along with it. Do what they need done; then finish something else. All the while, my feelings intensified.

I'm wondering how much of this is my own doing; my need for control. Since it's starting to bother me, does that mean I need to control less of my environment? "Hey, everyone! Do your own stuff. I no longer need to do it for you to feel in control and safe." I'd probably better show 'em how to do it first, eh?

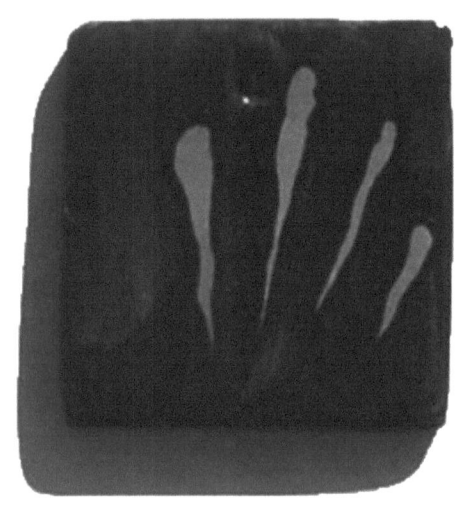

# December 15

Question of the day: What does your cage look like?

I have been thinking about it all day. What does it look like? Trying to "see" the walls – what color are they? Are they made of one way mirrors? Or glass? What's its shape? My house? My yard?

Duh. My cage is me. Those feelings of self-doubt, worthlessness. The sirens of my cage are the negative voices that I listen to – the harsh, belittling words. My fear keeps me inside instead of exploring the world and people in it.

My cage looks like the woman in the mirror. Nobody's holding me down, holding me back but myself. I am my cage.

## December 17

The end of the year is coming...time to start thinking about New Year's Resolutions.

I think before I make any new goals, I ought to acknowledge how much I've changed this year. Talk about improving my lifestyle! And, I bet, if I look close enough I will find that I am still doing learned behavior; thoughts and behavior that no longer fit with who I am now.

Dropping or changing, at the very least, acknowledging stuff that's no longer authentically me would make a great goal for the New Year!

## December 18

Sometimes words hurt just as much as an actual hit. They can certainly "draw blood."

Words can act as a trigger, just as certain smells can bring back a place or a stranger's gait makes you think of another man.

Certain words make me feel small, insignificant, stupid. I know in my heart that I'm none of these things but once I hear them, it's a very short leap to feeling the worthlessness. At times, I feel trapped by these emotions. Like today.

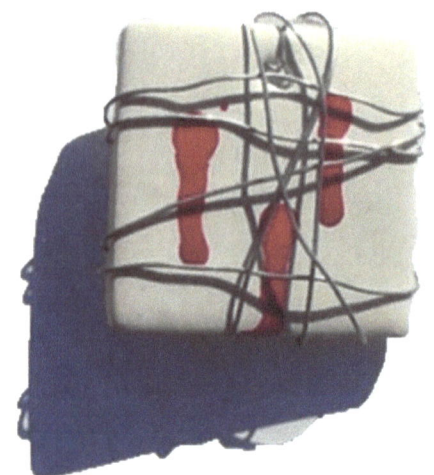

## December 20

Twenty three years ago today, I woke up. It's the first memory of awareness I have after the assault in October.

I awoke to pain, blood. So much blood! I used so many towels trying to mop it up. It was seemingly everywhere. The pain I was feeling was only overshadowed by my fear. Nobody must know! Shhhh, don't make a sound – not one peep.

And I never did. I never spoke of the utter grief I felt at holding my daughter's tiny little body in my arms. Of rocking her and sobbing.

I've never talked about being terrified as I wrapped her in a towel, knowing that I had to hide her, keep her safe. Bury her.

I wanted to die with her! But, at the same time, I was petrified that if I did die, everyone would know my secret. Everything. I would be exposed.

I never said a word. Not about the terror, or the despair, or the guilt or the all-consuming grief.

Until today. I love you, baby girl. I miss you with every beat of my heart.

## December 21

Family is supposed to love and support you, unconditionally. Friendships are supposed to be forever.

Then there is real life. Family members judge you, blame you, punish you or just completely turn their back to you. Friends lose your number, "unfriend" you or simply disappear from your life.

But just maybe, hopefully, you have an ally. A friend that shows up for you every day. Who not only sees you for who you are; she truly loves you and accepts you as is. She is not afraid to witness your pain; in fact, she will plop right down to sit with you in it.

To my friend: You are my family.

## December 27

Two days of crazy, five days of bouncing from total overload of emotions to a total lack of them has cost me. I am spent. Totally emotionally, mentally, physically and spiritually drained.

But I am present and being gentle with myself. And because of that compassion, fluidity came back. I felt frustration, accomplishment, annoyance, anticipation and joy pass through me.

I simply acknowledged each one, held it close then let it go. Beautiful.

## January 3

Ouch, that hurt. I asked a family member for support for the decisions I am making. Instead, I got an ear full of judgment, accusations and belittling comments.

Yes, it hurt me deeply. I felt rejected, abandoned, and disappointed.

Yet, I am tremendously glad I asked. I deserve to be surrounded by people who support me. They don't have to agree with my choices but they do need to acknowledge and respect my right to choose.

Afterwards, I did a body scan. Even with the sad feelings flowing through me, there was a settled feeling inside me as well. A rightness. The choices, the decisions I am making right now are not meant to harm or embarrass others. They are not selfish. They are simply choices I am making to live an authentic life, congruent with *my* views, values and desires.

### December 10 (a year later)

I once told a friend,

"You're living a beautiful life; I'm just trying to stay alive another day."

Living a beautiful life is more than just physically surviving a sexual assault. It is tending to the mental, spiritual and emotional wounds as well.

I've spent the last year working hard; identifying, acknowledging and sitting with any feelings or emotions I may experience. It's been a sometimes excruciating experience but also one filled with hope and gratitude. I have been more present and actively engaged this year than any other year of my life.

I have made enormous strides in my healing; my journey to awareness. Yet, the one thing I have truly learned is that it's a daily thing. I must check in with myself each and every day. I must greet and celebrate each emotion I have then simply let it flow away. Because when I do that, I can own that day; this day with these emotions.

I understand that even with the ending of The Pendant Project, my emotional healing continues. The acceptance and kindness I have learned to give myself is fundamental to building and increasing my awareness. Through compassion and awareness, I will start to live more authentically in my actions and emotions.

My beautiful life has begun.

www.ingramcontent.com/pod-product-compliance
Lightning Source LLC
Chambersburg PA
CBHW041551220426
43666CB00002B/37